UNSTOPPABLE
Success

UNSTOPPABLE Success:

How to FINALLY Create the Body, Business, & Lifestyle YOU WANT

TaVona Denise

While the author has made every effort to provide accurate telephone numbers and Internet addresses at the time of publication, neither the publisher not the author assumes any responsibility for errors, or for changes that occur after publication.

ISBN:978-0-9969104-0-8

Discounts for bulk sales are available. Please email Unstoppable@TaVonaDenise.com with inquiries.

DEDICATION

Mom – who has always had my back so I could fly…

Dad – the shining example of positivity and ambition…

My little bro – your success knows only the limits you place upon it…

Shine on…

Connect with TaVona Denise on Social Media

www.Facebook.com/TaVonaDenise

www.Instagram.com/TaVonaDenise

www.Periscope.tv/TaVonaDenise

www.Twitter.com/TaVonaDenise

www.Pinterest.com/TaVonaDenise

www.YouTube.com/TaVonaDenise

TABLE OF CONTENTS

ACKNOWLEDGMENTS

Thank you to those who have masterminded with me, on this, my largest project to date: Rolly, Taurea, Shan, and Nicky Pink. So glad you hopped on the roller coaster with me. And Adrienne, oh Adrienne. Thanks for being brave (or should we say naïve!) enough to walk into the fire with me.

To my editorial team:
Adrienne who got me started and did the heavy lifting with me. Roland, I knew your in-depth reading style would come in handy one day. Thank you for your patience and diligence in helping me finish what I started.☺. Mom & Ms. Melvina and your blasted red pen. ☺ I couldn't have done it without your mastery of words, catching my slip-ups, and polishing this gem into the beauty she turned out to be.

Your Personal Invitation

What is that thing that you really want to achieve? If, after reading this book, you are interested in additional support and want to improve your success rate, then I'd like to help you do it with a special one-on-one "Unstoppable Success" coaching session where we'll work together to...

- Create a crystal clear vision for "ultimate success" so you know exactly what you want, where you're headed, and what you need to do to make it happen.
- Uncover hidden challenges that may be sabotaging your ability to make changes that last or that are slowing down your progress.
- Leave you renewed, re-energized, and inspired to finally achieve the change you want - once and for all.

There is no cost and no obligation for the "Unstoppable Success" Session. I would be happy to discuss your situation, explain how I can help and how we can work together to achieve your goals (or I can connect you to the right resource). To apply for a session, please go to TaVonaDenise.com or email me at Unstoppable@TaVonaDenise.com.

In addition to the complimentary session, I offer coaching, tips, inspiration, online workshops and seminars to help you thrive in business and in life. All of which you can find at www.TaVonaDenise.com.

To book me for speaking engagements at your next conference or workshop, please contact me directly at Unstoppable@TaVonaDenise.com and tell me about the event you are planning.

PREFACE

Many people don't read the preface of a book. I know I usually don't, but for those of you who chose to start here, I thought I'd tell you how the book came about.

A series of events happened all in the span of 4 days really pushing me over the edge into action. I had been told, "You need to write a book." I wanted to, but I put it off. You know the usual excuses, *I don't have time. I don't know enough. Etc., etc.*

I had the occasion to go to a workshop on a last minute invite. It was led by a young lady that I had met at an event a year earlier. I vividly remember our conversation. She was so full of personality, had just finished her book, and was telling me how she did it in 30 days.

Sounded simple enough, but sometimes the mind likes to complicate things. It comes up with reasons you can't do something, so I pushed the thought away.

I didn't see her again.

When I saw the banner for the workshop event, I was excited. I instantly remembered our conversation about the book and realized I should have listened. But you know what? It wasn't my time.

During the workshop this young lady explained, in detail, the process of writing her book. This time, I was fired up!

Three days later I was sitting in my first mastermind meeting with people who have thriving online ventures. As I looked around the table, I saw one man who had just returned from training people in Silicon Valley (so you know what kind of money was being thrown around over there) and he remarked, "We're thinking too small."

Now, I'm the newbie in the group and I was already impressed with the fact that I was sitting across from someone who was paid to teach what he knows to that caliber of people.

Then another person sitting next to me said, "You're right. My highest month has been $100,000 and they looked at that like, *oh, that's cute.*"

What?! $100,000 a month?! Not a huge CEO, not an entertainer. A regular dude in jeans and a tee shirt, making $100K a month from his laptop.

My mind was split *wide open.*

I liken it to the story of the man that broke the 4 minute mile. At first they said it couldn't be done. Then, they said if it could, it would have to be a person with a build the exact opposite of the man attempting. Oh, but he did it, and people saw it was possible. Now people run a sub-4 minute mile all the time.

Towards the end of the meeting, one of them looked at me and asked, "What makes you *gangsta*?"

Huh?

After just a split second passed, I felt like I had an out-of-body experience as I heard myself respond, "I get what I want because I don't quit."

I just said *what*?! Shocked at my answer, I finally knew what drives my success.

People ask me all the time *how did you do this* and *how did you do that*? I tell them the steps, but if I am really honest with them and myself, I get what I want because I don't quit. Les Brown, motivational speaker and author, was the one that said it first and said it best, **"It's not over until you win"**, and that spoke to me deeply.

This book is my love note to your truest self. The one who knows no fear, hurt or anger. The one who knows that anything is possible and is actually living in that possibility. The one who is on the road to success and will not be stopped.

I invite you to consider the question, "What makes you *gangsta*?" and share it with us.

Admitting that to yourself and to others will make you *unstoppable*.

INTRODUCTION

"Success is 80% mental and 20% skill." – TaVona Denise

I used to think that if I did exactly what I was told, I would achieve my goals. And I did. I was the girl the coach could just tell me what to do, and I did it. I was vigilant about following the rules - the instructions - and I could get results. But I could only sustain the process for a while before the weight came back or my business failed.

If it was as simple as "eat less, exercise more", we would have less people worried about their weight. And if it was as simple as getting a business license, or a website, and the floodgates of customers came pouring in, we would have more millionaires.

In *Unstoppable Success*, I'll show you how I learned to create lasting success even after past failures. If you want to create sustainable results, you need to understand and incorporate the habits and skills that lead to success. Without them, you will struggle.

I'll tell you the story of how I finally figured out how to lose weight and keep it off, and how I applied those principles to building a lifestyle business.

In the following chapters, we'll take a look at how you can apply what I learned to creating success for yourself. We'll talk about the power of decision, overlooked, but so powerful.

We'll cover getting in the zone, setting yourself up for success with goals, preparing for obstacles, and dealing with self-doubt. Realizing that struggle is a part of the deal leads us to learning the how to create lasting change. Knowing that you can't do it alone means you need to know how to use masterminds, mentors, and coaches to succeed. And climbing the wall...fear – because it will stop you every time if you don't know to look and prepare for it. Finally, we'll address the dreaded plateau, and how to stay motivated on your way to success.

Each chapter provides you with a key piece of the process that I discovered through multiple fails - trial and error.

Don't quit until you win. This is the ultimate secret to success that doesn't stop.

CHAPTER 1

If At First You Don't Succeed...My Story

Have you ever tried to lose weight? How many times? Once? Twice? How about three or four times - or more?

How about building a business? Was it successful?

Maybe you're a black-and-white kind of girl. Either you're all in -doing everything you are supposed to - or you're completely out.

You may be able to motivate yourself long enough to make some changes, but why won't they last? How do you stay motivated? What is your real inspiration for doing what you're doing?

I gained and lost weight six or seven times before I finally discovered the steps to lose the weight and keep it off. Then as I built my own business, I applied similar steps to build momentum, get traction, attract clients, and start making money. I realized that the principles of success are the same whether you apply them to your body, your business, or your life.

Failure is not final. In fact, failure is necessary. It shapes our experiences and prepares us to walk in our purpose – to step into our greatness.

Pronoia is the belief that the universe is conspiring to support you. Everything that's happening now is ultimately to sustain you in achieving your goal - doing what you are meant to do, and being the best version of yourself. Beliefs like this give successful people their momentum and traction.
But we all meet failure and disappointment at times.

I was up for a supervisory position at a hospital. I love working with people, and organizing and leading. I had been working as a physical therapist for a while and had all of the qualifications necessary for this new opportunity. I felt the job was a good fit for me. There were interviews with current supervisors as well as peer reviews and interviews. The whole process went quite well. I just knew I had it!

However, I did not get the job. At first it stung, but then I thought, "What's next? There has to be a reason I didn't get this position. There's something else I'm supposed to be doing now."

And if I had been hired for that position, where would I be now? Certainly not writing this book -certainly not talking to you - certainly not on the path to living the life I knew I could create.

Think about the last time something didn't work out the way you wanted. Is it possible that the universe was conspiring something bigger and better for you? I lost weight over and over, and I kept gaining it back. I lost the same 50 pounds three times before I figured out something better - how to create a healthy lifestyle.

I gained weight, eating to fill a void that could not be filled by anything other than walking in my purpose. I was literally eating anything, and everything. Anything to distract me from the fact that I was not doing what I felt called to do.

What would life be like if more people had the courage to follow their own path? Would there be the need to distract with food, with alcohol, with sex, with drugs, with working, if we were really following our passion and really walking in our purpose?

One day I stood on the scale and it read 224 pounds. I could not believe I had let myself get to that point. It was the highest weight I had ever been. Having been an athlete in high school and college, I was ashamed of myself. I was appalled that I had let myself go. But it was also at that point that I made a decision that I wasn't going to travel down that path anymore. I could not continue. My knees hurt. I was tired all the time. I couldn't not shop in the stores that I wanted to shop in. I just did not feel good overall. I knew I was using food to fill a gap that needed to be filled another way. And I had had enough. I was going to figure out how to get rid of the weight – and keep it off!

I knew how to lose weight - I just didn't know how to keep it off. When I gained weight the first time and tried to diet, I was super strict. In fact, to this day I can tell you what I ate because I ate the same five meals every day for three months! Then when I "finished" the diet, I couldn't wait to eat everything I had been missing! And I gained it all back. I have gone to extremes to lose weight, like eating 500 calories a day and only strawberries, apples, and grapefruit, in exchange for fast results. Yes, I lost 55 pounds in three and a half months with HCG, but I don't recommend it. The weight came back - with a vengeance!

I could be successful losing weight. I knew it. But this time, I decided to not be so strict with myself that when I reached my goal-weight, I thanked God I wouldn't have to do it anymore, then make a 180 and gain all the weight back.

I made the decision to go to Weight Watchers® on my mother's recommendation. My mom and my aunts always went to their meetings and we had to sit outside and wait for them to come out. Weight Watchers® to me was a vision of old women in spandex, celery and carrots. And I had been there - I had done that. But at that time Jennifer Hudson was the spokesperson. She was younger. She looked like me. It was worth another try.

I told myself this time I have to be able to eat real food. I have to be able to eat potato chips and have margaritas along the way. I became aware of better techniques and started paying attention to what I was doing - but to the extreme. I became fanatical about counting my food and earning activity points just so I could eat more. It was still a control mechanism and it worked for the most part. I lost a lot of weight, but I struggled to keep it off. In my mind there were still distractions - what I should eat, what I shouldn't eat, how much I could eat, how much I needed to workout. There were so many rules and restrictions. I was following all of the rules, but there was still a void to fill.

It was a constant struggle - having to pay attention to what was going on. Why losing weight was so hard? Why was losing weight so hard???

I was doing what everyone else told me to do - I had not really become self-aware. I was looking outside of myself for clues – cues - as to what I should be doing. I wasn't listening to that voice inside that tells you what you need - your inner wisdom that tells you that "so and so" is no good for you - that tells you that you need to rest - the one that tells you, "Hey! You left that door unlocked."

I wasn't aware of how food – and thinking about food - was affecting my body. I was oblivious to my eating outside of weighing and measuring everything. I had no idea how my thoughts about the whole process were affecting my results.

You might be asking, "Great! But, what does that have to do with building a business?"

I realized that I had similar experiences to losing weight the first time I tried to build a business. My mentors would tell me, "You need to go out and meet people, network, follow up, show the plan, do all these things." I did what they said to do, much like I did with the losing weight. I was very meticulous about following the rules in the beginning. But then when it came to maintaining the process, it was a struggle. I wondered why. I lost the momentum to follow up. I would do certain parts of the process and not others. I just felt stuck – no traction - like I had no way to dig myself out.

I had done this before. I started two businesses straight out of college but burned out. I had the entrepreneurial bug. I had the dream of freedom and I had businesses that could support that dream, but they weren't my passion. They weren't something that I really loved to do. They didn't really speak to my soul, to my spirit, and ultimately my purpose in this world.

I was introduced to this incredible book called *The 4 Hour Workweek,* by Tim Ferriss, and my dream of freedom was ignited again but I didn't know how to apply the action steps in my life. I was without the guidance I needed. And I found myself $60,000 in debt.

I became discouraged. I wanted the vision that Tim Ferriss talked about. I wanted to be able to make money anywhere – from my computer, in my sleep – and travel the world with an income to support such dreams. And I was looking at the physical therapy contractor business I created - it was basically a j-o-b. I was trading hours for dollars. Making excellent money, but at that time, I also had a lot of debt to pay off.

I gave up on my dream of owning a virtual business temporarily to pay off debt with my traditional business. That meant that I had more time on my hands, and what did I do with time? I ate to fill the space - to fill the void - because I truly felt like a failure. I really enjoyed physical therapy, but it seemed like what I desired - the freedom to have a business where I could make money and work from anywhere - wasn't going to happen for me.

It wasn't that the techniques weren't working. I was being sabotaged by my own thoughts. Whenever something unpleasant happened, I blamed other people, or my situation.

I looked to everything outside of myself as the reason for my lack of success.

A turning point for me was the discovery that I had control over what I thought about situations in my life. I didn't have to let anything derail me. Entering life coach training and learning about power of our thoughts was pivotal. Up to that moment, I hadn't taken any responsibility for my own self. I wasn't listening to my inner wisdom. I was a victim. This didn't work and that didn't work and I tried what they said and I couldn't do it. It wasn't my fault I was unable to succeed!

I learned that I had the ability to choose what I thought about any situation that happened in my life. I didn't have to let it control me. And that was the key to getting rid of my last 30 pounds. They practically flew off of me! Once I started managing my mind - supervising my thoughts - I didn't need to run to food every time I had a bad day. I didn't need to control my food or keep certain foods out of my house. It was like a door opened up to me.

I used the principles in The 4 Hour Workweek and my weight loss to set me up for success, but the glue to make everything stick and click was to manage my mind. I use this principle in any situation. It's not what happens to us that matters – it's how we react to what happens to us.

It's going to be difficult at times. Getting rid of the weight was not a cake walk. Setting up a business isn't easy either. But what makes you keep going are the steps you put into place - the beliefs you have about your ability to succeed throughout the entire process. Once I tested that out with weight loss, I took those principles and applied them to business start-up.

Find something that you can commit to - something you're passionate about. In terms of losing weight, the key was finding something that would be an enjoyable lifestyle for me. For my exercise, I know I get bored easily so I had to mix it up. I have to like what I am eating. I need to continue to want to eat it – to find pleasure in my food. And with my business, it has to be something that fits my personality, something that I can stand behind, something that I could be proud of and passionate about.

After I realized I have control over what I think about any situation in my life, I decided to adopt the belief that things are always happening for me instead of to me. Imagine, finally discovering the system that helps you lose weight for good, to achieve the level of success you want in any area of life... Imagine finally knowing that you can be confident in your business, bounce back and smile - no matter what happens?

Apply the methods I outline in this book, and you will create lasting success for the goals you set for yourself. To help you design your success strategy, I have included written exercises and action steps to help you achieve your dream. Step by step, I will walk you through your journey to creating the lifestyle you desire. You will want to review your responses on a regular basis, so I have created a complimentary downloadable workbook that includes all of the written exercises and steps to *Unstoppable Success.*

All you have to do is go to my website (TaVonaDenise.com)

and download the *Unstoppable Success* Workbook so you can begin on your path to success. Go to it right now and download your free copy so you have it before we get to the good stuff.

Your first action step is to get your workbook.

Go ahead. I'll wait. Ready? Good – let's get started.

You will get a lot of information from reading a book, but the magic is in taking action. It's not the knowledge you have, but the knowledge you apply, that makes the difference.

Read the book, commit to the process, and watch yourself become unstoppable!

CHAPTER 2

Success Is An Inside Job:
Thoughts, Emotions, And Results

Nothing happens until you make up your mind.

This time I was serious. I could tell something was different. It felt different in my body. I was determined. I had been here before. I know this feeling well. It was like the time I decided to pay off some serious debt I had accrued from a business deal. When I made up my mind, I walked through, jumped over, and ran around everything in my way to pay off $60,000 in debt - in one year. I guess this is what the man was singing about in the Rocky movie. I had the eye of the tiger.

It had moved me before, but never like this. My usual M.O. was to get my act together, but only for a little while. I would go all in, for short periods of time, make some serious headway, then lose it all. I am a born sprinter. I don't have these big, powerful legs for nothing. Heck, they call me "The Rocket" in my cycling club because I can sprint with (and beat) the best of them. Yes, I ride with men.

In any case, I can tell when I've truly made up my mind. The energy is completely different and this time would be no exception. I had had enough of achieving a certain level of success then run 180 degrees in the opposite direction.

What was pivotal in that moment was the ***decision***. No more wavering. No more waiting (until Monday). No more thinking about it or *trying* to do it. I was *doing* it. So let's talk about why that was so important to my success and how it can help you.

When you decide that you're going to do something for real, failure really isn't an option. You're not going to half do it, you're all in. In fact, the root of the word decide is the Latin, –cide, which means to cut or kill off. Decide to do something and you are halfway there.

The decision alone is enough to get some people into action, but what happens after the excitement wears off? What helps some keep going and others quit?

"The way you think about anything is everything."
- TaVona Denise

There are people who for many reasons should not be successful, but they are. Maybe they weren't born into money, but now they are rich. Maybe they didn't have a college degree, but now they are the CEO of their own business. Or maybe they were born with a debilitating handicap, yet they just completed a marathon. They are successful. Why? How? Because they *choose* to look at their situation in a way that motivates them rather than tears them down.

On the other hand, you have people that for all intents and purposes should succeed: money, resources, support, education, looks, whatever, yet they are not successful. How is that possible?

What Gets in the Way of Success?

There are many things that can get in the way of success, but for most of us it is our thoughts. Our perception about our life and what happens to us. If you can understand what I am about to tell you, there is nothing and no one that can ever stop you from achieving success. Period. People ask how I got rid of the debt so quickly. They ask how I got rid of the weight and kept it off even after being unable to work out for months due to a back injury. This, my friends, is it.

But first, a little vocabulary lesson, because I want us all to be on the same page as I explain this.

Perception - a way of regarding, understanding, or interpreting something; a mental impression

Perspective - a particular attitude toward or way of regarding something; a point of **view** (meaning that there could be several and with additional information, the point of view could be changed)

Opinion - a **view** or judgment formed about something, *not necessarily based on fact or knowledge*

Thought - an idea or **opinion** produced by thinking

Think - have a particular **opinion**, belief, or **idea** about someone or something

Belief - an acceptance that a statement is true; an **opinion** or conviction

Notice a theme?

This is how it goes down.

1. Something happens or something just is (situation or circumstance).
2. We have an opinion about what happened (a thought runs through our mind about the situation).
3. This triggers an emotion (feeling).
4. We act or react based on how we feel.
5. This continued response over time creates our results.

People think that the way they think is reality. Unchangeable. That that's just the way it is and we are powerless to change it. And it is making them feel terrible and worse yet, keeping them in that situation. I would like to offer to you that you have a choice in the matter.

Let's look at the following examples: A car accident and getting fired

Situation: A car accident occurs (fact)
Thought: This is going to ruin my day (opinion)
Feeling: Frustrated
Reaction: Yell at the other driver
Result: Get into an argument

Situation: A car accident occurs (fact)
Thought: Thank God I'm not hurt (opinion)
Feeling: Relieved
Reaction: Check on the other driver
Result: Have a peaceful exchange

Situation: Got fired (fact)

Thought: I'm going to run out of money (perception)
Feeling: Depressed
Reaction: Sit on the couch all day
Result: No job = no money

Notice how this proves the original thought?

Situation: Got fired (fact)
Thought: Now I have time to work on my business (perception)
Feeling: Excited
Reaction: Start working on the business idea
Result: Build a business that creates more time

What's the difference?
A fact is something that can be proven in a court of law or by science. Everyone involved would say the same thing. It is 2 pm EST. There was a fire. She weighs 200 pounds. He is an engineer. The rest is a thought. An opinion. Something that can change. Meaning you get to *choose* how you want to think about anything that happens in your life.

Emotions

You can also change the way you feel by changing the way you think.

Notice how in both examples above, the situation did not change, only the way the person chose to think about the situation changed. When their opinion about the situation was positive, they felt a positive emotion. When their opinion about the situation was negative, they felt a negative emotion.

If you are feeling a negative emotion, you simply need to ask yourself, what am I thinking about right now? That will allow you to access the thought behind the emotion and allow you to change it, if you want to.

Think about a situation in your life that you would like to change. When you think about that situation, how do you feel? Do you feel frustrated or depressed, maybe defeated? Whenever you have a negative vibration or emotion in your body, it leads to negative results. The reverse is also true.

Here is a personal example:
My brother is 6 foot 2. I'm 5 foot 6. He wanted to gain weight. I wanted to lose it. At one point, we met in the middle at 200 pounds. When I stood on the scale and saw that number, all kinds of thoughts ran through my mind. *This sucks! I'll never be able to lose weight. No one will want me. How did I let myself go like this...*

When he stood on the scale and saw the number 200, he thought, *I've been killing it in the gym. What I'm doing is working. I'm finally going to be swole!* Those are the opinions that ran through his mind. The fact here is that we both weighed 200 pounds. Our individual thoughts made 200 pounds mean something very different.

When I chose to think that weighing 200 pounds meant something crappy, I let go of my dreams for happiness, love, a successful business. I felt ashamed and isolated. And when I felt like that, what did I *do*? Sit on the couch and eat. The result of that action was zero weight loss and even weight gain. It proved the original thought, *I'll never be able to lose weight.*

My brother chose thoughts – opinions about the circumstance - that made him feel excited. When he felt excited because he had thoughts of being swole, he continued go to the gym. The result was greater muscle mass. He proved his original thought, *I'm killing it! I'm finally going to be swole!*

The beautiful thing is the thoughts that run through your mind are optional. You get to choose what you think about any situation in your life. That truth is what brought me out of the funk and into positive action, creating positive results. You can take that principle and apply it to any aspect of your life.

Questions

Sometimes the thoughts come back in the form of a question. Why can't I get this right? Why does this keep happening to me?

The problem with this is the brain will search for evidence to support whatever you ask of it. So if you constantly ask yourself negative questions, your mind will go search for supporting thoughts which push you deeper in the rabbit hole.

Let's consider the question, why can't I lose weight? What answers might the brain come up with? *Because you can't run. You're lazy. You have no control around bread and pasta. And on and on.*

In your business, if you ask, why can't I get any clients, the answer may come back *because you suck at sales or there are too many people doing what you're doing.*

How can you shift the question to make your brain go to work for you instead of against you? Ask different questions. Tony Robbins says, **"Successful people *ask better questions*, and as a result, they *get better answers.***"

If you ask yourself, how can I make losing weight easier or more fun? You brain might come up with you like dancing, try that new class you have been thinking about. Try adding a vegetable to each meal, etc., etc.

If you ask yourself, *what do I need to do to make this business work?* The answer may come back, *tell why you do what you do to differentiate yourself. Start asking for referrals from your past clients,* and so on.

The interesting thing is when you put the question out into the world in the affirmative, it will not only return positive energizing answers, it will bring your awareness to resources and people. I can't tell you how many times I ask about how to do something in my business and all of a sudden, run across an article or video with the answer or meet a person at a networking function with the solution.

Your brain will go to work for you, if you let it.

Beliefs

Beliefs can be tricky, because they are usually deeply rooted, have strong emotional ties and are something a person has been thinking for a long time. However, if you remember the definition from earlier, a belief is an acceptance that a statement is true; an **opinion** or a conviction. This is good news. It means you can change them *if you want to*.

I love the story about the Roger Bannister, who was the first person to run a mile in less than 4 minutes. Prior to him accomplishing that feat, as legend has it, scientists said it couldn't be done, that it was physically impossible, that people had tried for a thousand years and couldn't do it.

The truth of the story is quite fascinating. The previous record of 4:01 stood for 9 years prior to Roger Bannister's attempt. He broke the barrier at 3:59.4 which expanded the minds of others. Within 46 days, another runner had beaten his record.

Your mind can be changed in an instant.

I wonder what John Landy, the second person to break the 4 minute mile, thought as he saw Roger Bannister do it? What new thought did he adopt that allowed him to now do the impossible? What thought can you adopt to help you do what you once thought was impossible?

It happened to me. For years, I never kept junk food in the house. I didn't trust myself. I thought I could not control myself around it, so it had to stay outside of the house. The problem with that thinking was, any and every chance I got, I ate junk food in the streets. Fast forward to me being near my goal weight. Still not keeping junk food in the house. Still not trusting myself.

During my study as a life and weight loss coach I learned to remove the labels "good" and "bad" from food. Of course there are foods that process better in our bodies than others, but where we get tripped up is in labeling those foods as bad. It's like the bad boy that we know we shouldn't date, but the temptation is just too great. We think we'll have more fun and just end up with more heartache.

The book, *Intuitive Eating*, introduced me to the concept of unconditional permission. I was used to control and moderation and the author was talking about giving myself unconditional permission to have what my body was craving. If it's chocolate, so be it, if cookies, so be it. To enjoy them while being aware of fullness within the body and stopping as a way to honor that fullness, not because I was trying to control something.

The key to it was in knowing that the food would not be taken away and was always available to me if I wanted it. I no longer felt deprived or tempted to overeat it, knowing that I could always go back for more if I wanted to.

It happened again with sales. I was terrified of asking people to work with me, asking for their business I would do it, because my coach told me to and I knew that I could not have a business without having clients, but my energy was all wrong. I was timid, I would accept any objection, leaving me without a new client, and them without the results they wanted.

Then I went to a class and the instructor said 'selling is sharing.' She asked us to consider the fact that if we had the cure for cancer would we tell people about it? Don't we tell people about other people's amazing products and services all the time? Why should it be any different when it comes to our product or service? It shouldn't be.

When you know the value of what you have to offer, all you are doing is sharing it with others. They get to say yes or no and that's okay too. This realization changed my mind in an instant. This new way of thinking and help me feel more confident about what I had to share. I was able to be more vocal about my services, which led to gaining more clients.

Actions and Reactions

If you noticed in the last two examples, what really drove my new behaviors (actions) was my emotions. With the food, I didn't feel deprived. With the business, I felt more confident. The thoughts made me *feel* a certain way, which drove the action.

When we are unaware of how we think about things, we cannot adjust how we feel. A person says something, we get ticked off, and it's off to the ice cream. It is like a knee-jerk reflex that we are powerless against because *they did this* to us.

However, when you realize that what *we thought* about what they said caused us to getting ticked off (the emotion) and go get the ice cream, we can change that. Again, really good news because we cannot change other people, we can only change ourselves.

The same goes for business. If we chose to think *networking is a waste of time*, we are likely to feel unenthusiastic and not follow up with prospects, resulting in fewer or no clients from networking proving the original thought, *networking is a waste of time*. However, if we choose to think, *there is a lot of opportunity in the room*, we are likely to feel excited and talk to more people which expands our network, possibly resulting in more referral business from the connections made at the networking function, proving the original thought, *there is a lot of opportunity in this room*.

Why Changing Behaviors Doesn't Work Long-Term

What people try to do, what I tried to do for many years, is to change the behavior to change the circumstance. I tried to eat less and exercise more without addressing why I was overeating and not exercising. I tried to go network without addressing why I didn't like sales. That does not work long-term.

When you find yourself going back to behaviors (actions) that you don't like, it is usually because you have not addressed the thoughts that created the behaviors in the first place.

Remember:
1. There is a circumstance or situation.
2. We have an opinion or thought about the circumstance.
3. This triggers an emotion.
4. We act or react based on how we feel.

5. This continued response over time creates our results.

In that order.

There are times where it *appears* that people were able to change their behaviors (actions), but what you don't see is how their thoughts also changed along the way. The thought *always* drives the action, never the other way around.

Where to Start

Start by being aware of the thoughts. Take the time to actually write them down or talk to someone so they can repeat your thoughts back to you. Often we don't realize how we are thinking about things until someone repeats it back to us. The thoughts swirl around in our head, wreaking havoc in our life and we have no idea what is going on.

When you write them down you can examine them for what they are and decide if you want to keep them or not. They are less "real" when written on paper. Less harmful.

A Word of Caution

We can be some of the meanest people to ourselves. Some of the things we say to ourselves, we would not even say to our enemies. When you start to observe your thinking, you may notice a lot of negative thoughts. Don't beat yourself up and approach this process with kindness and perseverance. If you allow the thoughts to come and just observe with curiosity, they will pass easier than trying to resist them.

The other thing I find is that when people become more aware, they see a negative thought and immediately want to change it. If you haven't taken the time to examine the various angles and thoughts that support your main thought, it will be difficult to get any real traction in changing it. What typically happens is people become aware of the negative thoughts, tried to flip the thought, don't see a change, get mad at themselves, and give up.

This, in my opinion, is why affirmations do not work for a lot of people. The brain is very efficient at its job. It collects a lot of evidence to support the thoughts that are there. For example, a person may think that they are not good at writing because they didn't do well in their English class, so they don't really attempt to try anything else related to writing. They avoid it like the plague, make no attempts to improve, so they continue to believe, *I'm no good at writing.*

When people create affirmations, they are usually written in the most positive form possible. I'm a rock star. I am a millionaire. I am beautiful. What happens is, the brain rejects the thought if it is too far from what they currently believe. It's too different from what it is efficient at thinking. It does not have the supporting thoughts to back that up. And the brain kicks it out.

What I recommend you do is to find something that is a little less painful or a little more positive that you *can* believe right now. If you are trying to build a business, maybe I'm a millionaire doesn't work for you, but I am getting better, I am learning more each day, I will figure this out…

It is a new skill that will require practice - work on a

consistent basis – but it gets easier. Just like lifting weights.

Success is 80% mental and 20% skill. Practice examining your thoughts and consciously choose the thoughts that serve you as go for your dreams. You'll be 80% of the way there.

For the other 20%? Keep reading. I'm going to show you more ideas that will support you on your path to Unstoppable Success!

"Happy are those who dream dreams and are ready to pay the price to make them come true." - Leon J. Suenens.

It's nice to want things and be determined to go after them, but let's talk about the steps to take to actually make that dream a reality.

CHAPTER 3

Getting in the Zone:
Goals, Obstacles, and Strategies

It's the day after Christmas and already I'm thinking about those dreaded New Year's Resolutions. They are the same as last year. Lose some weight, pay off some debt and go to church more.

December 26: *Another week then I need to make some changes, get myself together.*

December 31: *I'd better get it in because tomorrow I have to get it together.* I would write out all the things I needed to change and draw up a plan: Eat a salad for lunch every day, get up at 5:30 am and workout Monday-Friday, put $100 a week in savings and some extra toward debt.

January 1: *I'm going to be fit and fine this time.* I was excited. I would spend all day grocery shopping, packing my gym bag and laying out the first month's plan.

January 2: Things would come up. I wouldn't get to sleep early enough so the workout didn't happen. I didn't cut up the veggies after taking the time to buy them, so they went bad and I didn't have a lunch prepared, so I spent the extra money eating out.

I quickly fell back into old habits, felt like a failure and had trouble making progress. For years, this was me. And I suspect if you are reading this book, this has happened to you as well. Let's talk about why this typically doesn't work and what you can do instead.

Once we really make up our minds that a lot is not going right in our lives, we want to change it. All of it. At the same time. It's too much for us to take on at one time. It disrupts too many patterns and routines that we have in place and is frustrating, so it doesn't last for very long.

After many years of going at it that way, trying to get my entire life together on January 1st, I decided to go about it a different way. This time, I would break up the major goals. Establish some better habits in one area, then move on to the next.

I focused on *one* area at a time. The first year was financial health, the second physical health and the third spiritual health. The first year I paid off about $60,000 in debt, the second year I got rid of nearly 60 pounds, the third year, I established a spiritual routine that has made me healthier and happier. Here are the steps I took and what you can do to break the New Year's resolution cycle.

Get Clear About What You Want

It's pretty hard to hit the target if you don't know what you're shooting for. Many people have a vague sense of what they want, but haven't taken the time to define it and get discouraged when they haven't succeeded. Succeeded at what? Step one is to define what success looks like *to you*. Not anyone else.

For me, it was being able to lose weight and maintain a healthy lifestyle, while being able to have potato chips and margaritas. That was success for me. Yes, there was a number goal on the scale and a desire to wear a bikini, but including the occasional treats meant that I had to shift the way my mind saw success. I knew it might take longer than three months to lose the amount of weight I wanted. And I was okay with that. Being able to eat real food was just as important to me as the success of weight loss.

When you're creating your business – your lifestyle - what does success look like to you? Is it reaching a certain status or dollar amount? Replacing your current income or just being able to cover your expenses? Or is it creating a business that doesn't require you to trade hours for dollars? The point here is to be so clear and so specific about your goals that you can visualize them. Visualize yourself having achieved them. See yourself in the end zone, so to speak.

While it is very useful to visualize your success on a regular basis (I highly recommend it), it is even more important to write down your goals. Like the saying goes, out of sight, out of mind. If you are not continuously reminded of what you are supposed to be working on, it will be easy to slip back into what is easy, comfortable and familiar.

Why so many people resist this step, I don't know, but I have even noticed this in my own life. The goals that I write down and look at often, even if it's in the form of a vision board get accomplished much faster and more often than the things I do not write down.

Find Your Why

Do you want to know why some succeed and others don't? They have figured out the reasons that drive them to consistent action toward their goals. They have found a thought that motivates rather than demotivates them. Remember your thoughts determine your feelings which drive your actions (behaviors) which over time creates your results.

When you think about why you want to lose weight, what comes up for you? Do you want to do it because someone called you fat or you hate the way you look or you can't shop where you want to?

When you think about building a business is it because you hate your job or you feel like you don't have any choice or you don't want people to think you didn't live up to your potential?

How do these thoughts make you feel? I'm guessing that they don't feel very good. When we feel bad, we do bad. But what about the person who works out or runs when they have a rough day? What is the thought actually driving the action? Not *I had a rough day*. It's *working out makes me feel better*.

Find the thoughts that make you feel good, lean on them and you will be one step closer to achieving unstoppable success.

When I ask some clients what their why is, they say "I want to help people." Don't get me wrong, I love people and I want to help people, too. In fact, my mission is to help people make money who want to make a difference, right? But my **why** is about freedom. My why is about being able to get up when I want to, go where I want to, buy the things that I want to, travel where I want to, live where I want to. That's my real why. And then my second why is those other things.

It doesn't have to be something materialistic, like you don't have to want a Maserati or a Tesla, it could be something like having the peace of mind to know that you don't have to make decisions based on money, that your children can go to any school that they want to and you don't have to worry about telling them that you don't have the money.

The why is your fuel for action. And so people do not get up at 3 o'clock in the morning just because they want to help people. They don't work seven days a week. They don't work 8, 9, 10 hours on a job and then put in 4, 5, 6 more hours for their business because they just want to pay off a few bills. It's got to be deeper than that.

So make sure that your reason is so deep that it will make you get up in the morning and handle your business. It will make you get up and go to the gym when you don't really feel like it. That's the why that you're looking for.

The Best Way To Write Goals

Instead of saying *I want to lose weight.* Get specific. How much weight? In how much time? Instead of *I want to start a business and quit my job.* What type of business? By what date do you want to be able to walk away from your job?

Resolutions say *I want to lose weight.* Goals say, *I will lose 30 pounds by July 4th.* Resolutions say, I want to quit my job. Goals say, I will replace my W-2 income with income from my business by July 4th.

In each of the examples above, the goals are specific, measurable and time-based.

Use the <u>Unstoppable Success Workbook</u> to create some goals for yourself.

A goal without a timeline is just a dream. -Robert Herjavec

Break It Down

One client came to me saying, "I can't get anything done because everyone is always pulling on me! There is so much to do!" After digging deeper, we found that there were specific blocks of time where she could tackle things on her to-do list she was not taking advantage of. Breaking her big goal into smaller tasks helped her feel like she could be productive, even in small blocks of time.

Some people fail because they quit before they get started. They may see a goal like, make $100,000 when they haven't landed their first client or run a 5K (3.1 miles) when they can't walk a mile without running out of breath and psyche themselves out.

Whenever you are tackling a large goal, it is important to break the goal down into mini goals or benchmarks so you can see progress and know you are on the way to achieving the goal, rather than feeling like you have so far to go.

For example, you want to lose 50 pounds. If you work hard for a month or two, you are likely to still be quite a ways from your goal, but if you say, my goal is to lose 5 pounds, you can hit it and reset the goal until you eventually reach the larger goal. The same with building your business. If you want 10 clients, start by getting one. Eventually, you will learn what it takes to get to 10, then repeat.

When you look at your benchmarks on a regular basis, it then becomes very clear as to whether or not you're getting close to your objectives - and why, or why not.

The other part of breaking the goal down is breaking it into components. Take a look at where you want to be and ask - *how do I actually get there?*

Break it down in to the parts to achieve the goal. If you want to lose weight, there are two basic components: how you eat and moving your body. What strategies will you use to improve how you eat? What will you do to start moving your body?

In building a business there are several components: admin, finance, product or service delivery, marketing component and the sales component among other things. What things will you do yourself and which will you delegate?

Breaking down the components of the end goal makes it easier to see what is involved and you can decide what you want to do. The rest you can delegate or remove from your plate.

Be Honest With Yourself

There is no such thing as "time management". Time marches on, and we are left to determine what we do with that time. We have to learn how to manage ourselves. Do you have areas where you could do things differently, more efficiently, or more productive in same amount of time? Think about opportunities where you could be using your time more effectively. Is it that you don't have time or are you investing your time in things that are not important to achieving your goal? It's okay if that is what you're choosing to do, but be honest with yourself about it.

Your goals should direct the priorities in our life. Your priorities should determine what you give your time, attention, and energy to.

Peter Drucker, management consultant, educator and author, said, **"First things first, and second things not at all."** Part of this is taking a clear look at what needs to be done. Write it down. Take a look at the list. Do you personally have to do all of these things, or can something be delegated? Does it all have to be done right now? There may be a lot of things needing to be done, but they don't all need to be done immediately. Writing a to-do list and examining the items can make the process less scary - more manageable.

Now that you have a better idea of what it's going to take, you can look for the gaps. *What do I need to learn how to do? Who might I need to be connected with? What am I willing to do and what am I not willing to do?*

When I finally decided to lose weight for good, I was not willing to starve myself. I was not willing to go through the binge-starve cycle. What I *was* willing to do was slow down, be patient, try new things, work with mentors, and be consistent in my follow-through.

When it comes to your business, what are you willing to do - what aren't you willing to do? Are you willing to do what your mentors and coaches suggest? Are you willing to not quit or give up when it gets hard? Are you willing to give up television? What about social media? How about sleep? I decided I was not willing to give up sleep on a regular basis. I know that it is part of my health - being sharp and being able to function. But I am willing to give up television, going to the movies. Those were negotiable.

Based on your goals, what activities are a priority for you? Make space for the things that are priority for you first and then give time to the rest. You will reach your goals a lot faster than waiting to find time for what you say is important to you.

Anticipate the Obstacles

What may come up for you as you try to achieve this goal? Look at things like your schedule, other people, other activities, or your current routine. The trick is to anticipate the obstacles and come up with a strategy to overcome them.

I'll give you a prime example.

I don't like to get up early. As much as I try, I simply am not a morning person. So the only option for working out was after work. Problem was, I would be so tired after work I would drive myself and my gym clothes back to the house for months at a time. What I decided to do was to take the gym bag into my job with me and change before I left the building. To this day, I have never driven myself home in my gym clothes.

As I was starting my coaching practice, there was a lot to learn and do. A lot of times I felt guilty and unproductive when I was working out and couldn't give it my all because my mind was on work. So I decided to listen to podcasts and audiobooks while working out. That way I got two things done at the same time. I felt accomplished, so I continued to do it.

Accountability

I'll just be honest, when left up to my own devices, sometimes things just don't get done. I have learned that one of the best things you can do for yourself is to tell someone else what you are trying to accomplish. Prior to deciding to write this book, I thought about it, dreamed about it, even took classes on how to do it. Yet, it never got done. When I told people-lots of people-that I was going to write it and it would be out by a certain day, the deal was done. I *had* to write it. There was no way I was telling that many people that I was going to do something by a certain time without following through. It lit a real fire under my butt and that's what telling people can do for you.

Finally, when it comes to goals you can get some support. There are several different types of support, which we will cover in Chapter 5, but know that you don't have to, nor should you try to do it alone.

CHAPTER 4

How to Make Changes
That Last

The pain from the workout was excruciating. Getting in and out of a chair was difficult at best and I was walking like Frankenstein. I was only good about maintaining a workout routine for a few weeks before I fell off the wagon and reverted to my old habits. So every time I decided to go to the gym after a long hiatus, I had to suffer the consequences. Fast forward from the moment I made the decision that I would make health and fitness part of lifestyle and I have not missed a workout in 4 years. Let's talk about why it's so difficult for people to change and what you can do to make some serious changes in your life.

Why Is It So Hard to Change?

Change is difficult because we're hardwired for efficiency. It is how our brain functions. Its major purpose is figuring out the most productive way to accomplish our tasks with the least amount of energy.

There is a particular way you put on your pants, brush your teeth, drive to work. You can multitask – drive, talk on the phone, eat a granola bar - because your brain has made certain neural connections, making the process more efficient. That is also how habits are created. Efficient neural pathways and

connections develop and our task becomes "second nature" –
we run on "auto pilot". It no longer requires a lot of energy
or effort because our subconscious takes over the task.

We have to exert energy to break old neural connections and
establish new patterns. Some of my physical therapy patients
have had strokes. The connections on one side of their brain
have been disrupted. Movements are very weak,
uncoordinated and awkward as they begin to recover. It
doesn't take a lot of physical activity for them to become tired.
To walk just 10 feet is exhausting. Their brain is now using a
lot of energy to make new connections - new neural and motor
pathways - to complete the same movement that had once
been "second nature".

I have worked with a lot of women who believe *that's just the
way I am* and they can't change because *that's the way it's
always been.* They don't realize that our brain has the
capacity and the ability to form new pathways, growing and
learning until we die. We are created with the ability to flex
and adapt, but it can be frustrating when we initially attempt to
change.

Brooke Castillo, life coach and mentor, says **"Anything that
you are wanting in your life starts as that seed of desire. It
is your invitation to evolve."** If you desire to be, do, or have
something different, it is going to require you to stretch
beyond your current belief system and grow. It's not enough
to wish, pray, hope - you have to work for it. Remember
when it comes to wanting more for yourself in your life, you're
going to have to make some changes.

Think about science class again. Remember Newton's first law? An object in motion remains in motion until some force changes its path. An object that is at rest remains at rest until some force changes its status. If I'm sitting in a chair and I don't want to be sitting there anymore, what am I going to have to do? I can't keep sitting and think about getting up. I have to do something. I have to use energy. I have to use the strength in my legs – then, and only then can I get up from the chair.

When we want to be somewhere we are not currently at, we have to do something differently. Without that force we will continue to stay, in our chair, stuck. So how do we direct change? Change your thoughts, change your habits and commit to that change.

Change Your Thoughts

You have to get your mind right. Know what motivates you, what demotivates you and use it to your advantage. When something is not going the way you'd like, ask yourself, how can I make this work for me? Going after positive thoughts and examining the thoughts you have about the task at hand will support the changes you want to make. This is the first and most important step.

Change Your Habits

Sometimes the problem is that we try to take on too much at once. That, in and of itself, can be overwhelming. When I made my annual New Year's resolutions, I'd plan it all out and buy everything, trying to make too many changes at once, burn out and fail. Or perhaps you've said, "I'm going to do it this time. I'm starting that business." But once you begin and discover all of the moving pieces, you become overwhelmed and quit because you think it's too much. Has this ever happened to you? Maybe you're trying to change too much at the same time. Commit to one thing you know you can do, get the hang of that, and then add the next piece.

Once you are aware of what gets you into action and what stops you in your tracks, you want to make things easy for yourself. If you are a night owl, it might not be the best idea to schedule 5 am workouts or 7 am business meetings. I have never driving home with my gym clothes on, but I have driven them around in the back of the car for months at a time.

Build some flexibility into your schedule if you need to. I instituted a 2 day rule with myself that has worked like clockwork for the past 4 years. It goes like this - I can rest, skip, take on impromptu activities for 2 days, but on the third, I must do some type of physical activity for at least 20 minutes. This allows me to get in at least 3 workouts per week not matter how you slice it. It also allows me to have some flexibility without feeling like a failure if something comes up or I miss a day. Try it. I'd love to hear what you think.

Commit to the Change

One thing that has always fascinated me when I see it in myself as well as others is that we will get up and go to work when we don't feel like it, but we easily skip the gym or doing something in our business because we don't feel like it.

My question to you is can you commit to yourself, your goals, your success? This is much easier to do when you know your why. Author and Sales Trainer Brian Tracy said, **"you either work to achieve your own goals, or your work to achieve someone else's goals."** Which would you rather spend your life doing?

No, it's not always going to feel like peaches and roses. You'll get tired, frustrated. You will want to quit. But commitment is like the Two-Day Rule I explained earlier. Yes, sometimes two days have passed and I still don't feel like moving - but I've committed to myself, and to my goal of having a healthy lifestyle, so I get up and do it. The same goes for my business. If I have committed to coaching on certain days or networking or a certain number of sales calls, the show must go on if I am committed to having the lifestyle I want.

"Commitment means staying loyal to what you said you were going to do long after the mood you said it in has left you." - Orebela Gbenga

It's amazing how many solopreneurs and online business owners want to wait until the mood hits them to do certain activities in their business. When we had an employer, we would go to work when we didn't feel like it, get up and push through it for somebody else, but we won't do so for ourselves. What is the difference? You may think the repercussions of not going to work for an employer are worse than remaining in the comfort of your own bed. But it goes back to your why - your reasons - again.

What leverage can you use on yourself when you're feeling less than inspired? Sometimes it's as simple as remembering that you made a commitment to yourself, your clients, and potential customers. If you had a traditional brick-and-mortar business, you would put up the sign that says you're open Monday-through-Friday, 8:00 AM to 6:00 PM. Suppose you woke up and didn't feel like working that day? You can't say, *I'm not inspired to open the store today.* You go to work or you find somebody to open the store for you. It's no different with an online business. Even if we are the only one running the show, the same level of commitment should apply. Our success depends on our commitments.

CHAPTER 5

You Cannot Do It Alone:
Masterminds, Mentors, And Coaches

"Even the smartest geniuses can't build businesses alone."
Mark Zuckerberg, Facebook CEO

I had never gone 100 miles on my bike before. I was afraid. The most I had done was 66 miles and I thought that was tough. Adding 34 more miles would be interesting, to say the least. I was in the parking lot when a group of my cycling club members saw me. "Hey TaVona! You're doing the century with us, right? You've done enough metrics (62 miles/100 kilometers) already." I had almost escaped, but they caught me. I reluctantly moved to the section with my cycling club members who were about to ride 100 miles. Peer pressure is something else!

We mounted and took off in a double paceline where we rode two abreast. Talking, laughing and passing many other riders. I looked down to see us pacing at 20 mph. What?! I've never gone at this pace before. I'll never be able to keep this up for 100 miles. And I didn't. But I did maintain it for 50 miles without a rest stop. I even made it about 15 more miles before my legs said no more. I could not maintain that pace. I was dropped from the group. I was by myself fighting, taking the wind on my own. I fatigued very quickly and my average speed dropped down to 14 miles an hour. I was hurting and physically in pain because of the effort that I had to put out on my own.

When cyclists ride together, they either ride in a large group called a peloton or they ride in a single file line, called a paceline. These formations allow the cyclists to draft and 30 to 40 percent less energy is used when drafting off the rider in front of them.

Then a group of riders came up beside me. They had formed their own paceline and yelled for me to hop on. They pulled me. They pulled me so that I could benefit from them blocking the wind. It allowed me to recover. It allowed me to speed up. Eventually, I was able to get back into the front and pull the other riders. Average speed as we crossed the 100 mile mark? 18.4 mph. What I learned in that moment is that you can go faster and farther when you have people working with you and routing for you, then when you try to do it alone.

Masterminds

According to Napoleon Hill, in *Think and Grow Rich*, **"The master mind maybe defined as the coordination of knowledge and effort, in a spirit of harmony between two or more people, for the attainment of a definite purpose."**

When I think about the concept of masterminds, I think about everything I've learned as a cyclist about drafting. It's all about blocking the wind. The wind is like obstacles preventing us from reaching our goals and dreams.

In the paceline and peloton, we are talking to each other -

encouraging one another. When the person that's in the front blocking the wind for everyone gets tired, they fall off and go to the back. It is their turn to benefit from the draft. When the next person moves up in line, they are fairly fresh because they haven't been taking all the wind. This is the power of working with other people.

Belonging to a mastermind group has similar benefits. When you have questions and challenges come up, you can ask the group - lean on them for ideas and knowledge. They help you to grow and stretch. Masterminds provide constructive criticism and skills to avoid mistakes in the future. They also provide accountability and support. You are given opportunities for strategic partnerships - furthering the growth of both your businesses.

The people I ride with are stronger and faster than I am, which encourages me to go faster. They get me to ride when I don't feel up to it and ride faster and further when I don't feel like I can.

The people I met up with in my first organized business mastermind did the same thing for me. They asked me what my challenges were and I just watched the ideas fly. Brilliant minds from everywhere, that charged clients as much as $1,000 an hour, sharing their knowledge, wisdoms, and talents in a mastermind group. The energy is contagious. You can't help but to leave there fired up.

Finding a Mastermind

How do you find a mastermind? You can start by asking if

anyone in your network knows of one. You can also search for online forums. I tend to like the masterminds that are in person but you can participate in online forums where you get together via Google Hangouts or use a conference call service.

You can join masterminds with people that are in your same area of expertise, but I find it's more beneficial to be diversified – offering different perspectives and eliminating blind spots.

Another thing to be very careful of when you look at a mastermind is their level of organization. Are they very active? Is everyone committed to each other's success and growth? It should not be a group where everyone gets together and complains or whines about their challenges, and when you meet again, they still haven't achieved anything!

If you don't find a mastermind that you feel like suits your needs, create one. You will want to first decide what the intention is for the group, the guidelines, the common purpose. Remember the *why* to what you are doing.

Is this going to be a paid or unpaid mastermind? Some have great success with being unpaid – this version does not limit valuable participation. Yet at the same time, I have found in my business and coaching that having some skin in the game really increases the people's level of commitment. You have to decide which route you want to go. There are pros and cons to both.

How often will you meet and where will you meet? Is it a weekly meeting? Is it a monthly meeting? Are you meeting in person or virtually? How long will the meetings run? It determines how many people can participate - you want to give everyone a chance to be in the "hot seat" and get their challenges addressed.

Make a list of those you would think will be a great fit for a mastermind. Is there somebody in particular that you feel really connected with that has similar goals to you? Is there someone with a similar level of ambition that you know would be rooting for you, and not let you quit on yourself? Remember, a mastermind can be as few as two people.

If you decide to start your own mastermind group, the first time around you may want to make it for a specified, short period of time. Try it out for three months, for example, then reevaluate and determine if it should continue. Some members will naturally exit the group. Will new people be invited to come in, still keeping it small enough where everyone gets a chance to participate and be heard?

There are lots of resources that you can look up in order to formally organize your mastermind, but there is a very basic format for the meetings. Each person gets a turn in the "hot seat" - the spotlight is on them for a designated amount of time. Discuss what the "win's" are, what challenges are still being faced, and the goals and action steps to take before the next meeting. You can set up a Facebook group for accountability and resources, and collaboration in-between the calls or meetings.

The Right People

The interesting thing about success is it doesn't happen in a vacuum. It doesn't just happen when you're on the court, but more likely in between. John Rohn, entrepreneur, has said, **"You are the average of the five people you spend the most time with."** Who are your five people? Are they mostly positive people or are they negative? Do they complain about money? Do they eat healthfully or not? Do they watch a lot of TV? What podcasts are they listening to? Music? Books? It really makes a difference in your life.

Also consider their income. If you want to make more money, make sure the people you invest your time with make the kind of money you want to be making. Ask yourself if you see a pattern in these people. Do you need to make some changes?

When I first encountered the cycling club on my weight loss journey, we met at a restaurant. I noticed that everyone was eating healthfully – fish, chicken, vegetables, whole grains. In that situation, I would have felt foolish to order French fries. Just by virtue of being around these other cyclists, I wanted to step up my game - to keep my eating clean, because that's how they roll (pun intended).

When it comes to reaching your goals, take a look at the people you have surrounded yourself with. You may notice several that you should probably consider separating from. If you decide to stay connected to them, is it worth delaying - or not achieving *success* - in your goals? You know in your gut what the best decision for you is.

When you are going on a certain path and your goals and priorities have changed, the people you surround yourself with will change. That's normal. There will be a time when you need to disconnect from the things that you were doing and the people that you were doing those things with in order to get to a certain place in your life. It's part of the process. Have the courage to move forward.

Mentors

Aligning yourself with the right people will get you to success faster than doing it alone - even if you are self-motivated. This book would not have been written without a push. I heard about the 30 day book writing experience 3 different times, but it wasn't until I was actually in one of the author's circles that I actually pushed myself to get it done. I wasn't off by myself for a year and a half - left to my own devices and thoughts of *one day...*

Sometimes we need somebody else being in our space - knowing what we said we would do - to hold us accountable. Learning how to connect with the right people boosts our chance of sustained success, and minimizes the learning curve.

One of the most important things you can do is surround yourself with others going where you want to go - people who will not let you quit on yourself. I've had many mentors in my life. They have had a vested interest in me as a person. Some were paid to mentor and some were not. It was casual and laid back, with some relationships lasting for longer and others for shorter periods of time. Mentors provide advice and offer their expertise. They are focused on your personal growth and are more experienced and qualified in the area you wish to pursue. I've also called someone a mentor who I have had the occasion to meet and/or study their works.

Choosing a mentor

Finding and choosing a mentor tends to happen quite naturally. I've been mentored through books, podcasts, and classes. But sometimes, for one-on-one mentoring, you have to be proactive and ask. You want to reach out to someone you admire and let them know you appreciate their work. Tell them what you're trying to accomplish and ask if they will mentor you. You must ask for what you want or the answer will always be no.

Consider being a mentor, as well. When I mentor others, it keeps me sharp – often they ask questions that I need to know the answers to. Giving of your time and energy always comes back to you.

Coaches

When beginning a business, sometimes your vision is hard to pin down and express. You need to talk to someone with the unbiased view. You have a goal that you want to achieve and you need someone to hold you accountable to your goals – someone to help you navigate the blind spots. A relationship with a coach is usually for a specific period of time, or a specific goal, and the setting is more formal. Typically, it is a paid arrangement. A coach is to hold you accountable to what you say you wanted to do and to help you find the best you have to offer.

In addition to holding you accountable, my job as a coach is to show you your mind. I show you how your thoughts are affecting your actions and creating your results. I help you find your internal wisdom, hold you accountable, and help you see and display the best version of yourself. I'm a very analytical person - I love how things work. I do some consulting (providing advice) and strategy, but as a coach, when you're not taking action or getting the results you want, I get in there with you. Together we figure out what's going on at a deeper level.

Choosing a coach

There are many different types of coaches and schools of thought. Some of them are more about giving advice and strategy – consulting. But there are others that use questions to access your inner wisdom. When choosing a coach, find out what type of coaching they offer and make your selections based on what you need. Can they coach you on issues of fear, frustration, overwhelm? Do they use a softer touch or do they just cut to the chase when they're coaching you? Can you relate to them in their personality and approach? What services do they provide? Do they provide coaching, advice, accountability, and resources? Do they help you implement the plan once it's in place?

What do you need most *right now*? There are many different coaches and different niches. Do you need a health coach? Do you need a weight coach? A money coach or a business coach? Do you need more than one type of coach? Have they been where you want to go? Or are they headed in the same direction? Sometimes it's better to go with someone two or three steps ahead of you versus twenty. Sometimes that is too big a gap. Do they remember what it was like just starting out because they are so far removed now? Do they assume that you know certain things because they do? Look at their testimonials – what are people saying about them and their results from working with them? Do they typically work with people in your specific situation?

I work with other coaches and people in service-based businesses, particularly women who want to have online/location-independent businesses. And I've had people come to me who want to start product-based businesses. While I can provide some strategy, I would be doing them a disservice to say that that is my area of expertise. That is not my Zone of Genius so I will refer them out. You will want to take all of these things into consideration when choosing your coach.

CHAPTER 6:

The Wall: Fear

Will you Forget Everything And Run or Face Everything And Rise?

I was sweating like crazy, my heart was pounding and there was a tightness in my stomach. I thought I was going to be sick. I knew getting on that stage would be a serious boost for my business, but I was afraid. The thoughts started flying. *What if this? What if that? What if...?*

I wanted to be on that stage. I wanted to tell my story. My grandmother's words moved to the forefront of my mind as I could hear her singing, *if I can help somebody as I go along, then my living shall not be in vain.* I took a deep breath and stepped onto the stage and the words flowed from my lips. When I finished, the applause was loud. Throughout the afternoon, women kept repeating parts of my speech. They were listening. My words touched them. I didn't get sick after all.

Just like any other emotion, we can create fear with our thoughts. Just like we can create excitement, we can create fear. Usually the "what ifs...?" You can fill in the blank with all sorts of things and it will scare the crap out of you. Our thoughts are real *in our minds*. They create real physiological responses. Bill Baren, Business Coach says, **"fear comes from thinking about the game instead of being in the**

game." That's why it's so important to get the thoughts out of your head and on paper.

Let's just address a few of the most common fears that interfere with our goals: Fear of failure, success and rejection.

Fear of Failure

For years I struggled with depression because I was not going after my goals. I had failed at some really big goals before and I was afraid to try again. I got stuck in survival mode, doing the status quo. I wasn't going after anything that really lit me up because I was afraid of failing and the fear of failure had me paralyzed. However, going big, stretching, reaching and sometimes failing keeps us moving forward. I notice that when I really go for something with all my might, I feel the most alive.

We fear failure. We keep ourselves from doing so many things that could help us grow because we don't want to look silly. We don't want to be unsuccessful. But what is failure really? FAIL is simply your **F**irst **A**ttempt **I**n **L**earning. What might you do differently if you thought about failing like that?

Author, C. Joybell C. says, **"Don't be afraid of your fears. They're not there to scare you. They're there to let you know that something is worth it."** And that's huge! If you think about it, the things that don't matter don't really bother us. They don't keep us up at night. They don't occupy our thoughts for very long. The things that really matter to us are the ones that freak us out and make us doubt ourselves like, *what if I don't get it right?*

Can you be okay with your results not looking like you expect them to at first? Are you willing to try a few things in order to find your sweet spot? I lost and gained weight many times before I found out what methods actually worked for me. I started three businesses before I found the one that really put me in my Zone of Genius.

Ambrose Hollingworth Redmoon, writer and former band manager, said, **"Courage is not the absence of fear, but rather the judgment that something else is more important than fear."**

It takes courage to try something new and be committed to the outcome. Where does that courage come from? It is not a gift that some have and others don't. The quickest way to build courage and confidence is to *get into action.* How do you know you'll be good at something until you do it? It goes back to knowing your brain has the ability to adapt and learn new things – it improves with practice.

Are you confident you can lift a heavy weight or do you need to attempt to do it first? Are you confident can you run a 5K before you try? Coaching, sales calls, and anything that is required of you in your business will improve with time, but you have to get started first and have the courage to get started, make mistakes, learn from them and keep going.

What is it you've been avoiding out of fear that will make all the difference if you just did it? What step can you take *today* to get closer to your dream?

Perfectionism

At one point in time, I was a straight-A student. I know what it's like to want to be right - to get it right and not look like a fool. I wanted to make sure I knew all the "ins and outs" and how everything worked. I was stuck in the cycle of wanting to know everything and making it perfect before I put anything out there. I read everything that I could get my hands on. I studied everything I could find to have all possible knowledge at my disposal. I was doing a little bit of activity, but "learning-mode" doesn't build a business.

Perfectionism grips us and then it paralyzes us. We think everything has to be in order before we put ourselves out there. We don't realize that the people drawn to us will be drawn to us no matter what. Our typos and our mistakes may be visible, but if our information is solid, then our clientele won't care. And sometimes, they don't even notice. People connect more with real people - who have flaws, that make mistakes. Our human-ness actually endears people to us.
The only way to get feedback and improve is to *get started.* We sit on things under the guise of "I'm trying to figure it all out first" but we never "figure it *all* out". We learn *enough* and then we need to get going. Then we learn more, coming up with the next iteration of the process.

Are you willing to *not* get it right at first? Are you willing to suck at lifting weights? Are you willing to start by lifting 5 pounds? Try saying, *At least I can lift five pounds today. I wonder what I'll be able to do tomorrow.* Jeff Calloway, former Olympic runner, teaches people to run *marathons* by running 30 seconds and walking 15 seconds in a repeated pattern. Running 30 seconds at a time can lead to a marathon! So what else is possible?!

Are you willing to make yourself and your business visible - tell people what you do? Are you willing to come up with your mission statement and share that out loud? Can you handle when someone looks puzzled because they don't quite understand? That is the feedback you need to improve your communication about your business. Without trying – without attempting to share your mission statement - you won't have feedback. Nobody will know what you do and why you do it!

Ray Edwards, marketing strategist and author, says, **"Done is better than perfect, because perfect never gets done."** Are you willing to walk your purpose and let "good enough" be *good enough*? Can you choose to let "done" be *done enough* in order to discover the responses and grow? Are you willing to stumble, knowing that it's only a matter of time before you achieve success?

Fear of Rejection

Nobody likes to be rejected, but it's a part of the deal. One of my mentors, Brooke Castillo says, you can be the sweetest, juiciest peach and there are going to be people who simply don't like peaches. (And it's okay.)

Critics

There will be critics. One of my favorite quotes is from

Theodore Roosevelt's speech, "The Man in the Arena".

It is not the critic who counts; not the man who points out how the strong man stumbles, or where the doer of deeds could have done them better. The credit belongs to the man who is actually in the arena, whose face is marred by dust and sweat and blood; who strives valiantly; who errs, who comes short again and again, because there is no effort without error and shortcoming; but who does actually strive to do the deeds; who knows great enthusiasms, the great devotions; who spends himself in a worthy cause; who at the best knows in the end the triumph of high achievement, and who at the worst, if he fails, at least fails while daring greatly, so that his place shall never be with those cold and timid souls who neither know victory nor defeat.

And there will be "gremlins". Brenè Brown talks about "gremlins" in her book, *Gifts of Imperfection*. Not the 80's movie creatures, but it is a really good analogy - some thoughts or beliefs seem soft, cuddly, and innocent until you water them. The "gremlins" here are our internal dialogues while the critics, from above, are external.

We can examine and silence our "gremlins", by changing the way we think, but it is more difficult with critics. We have no control over what other people say or do. But we can allow people to be who they are going to be and not allow it to affect what we do. In the end, they don't pay your bills. They don't have to live your life. Know that anytime you put yourself out there, *doing* something that is important to you, not everybody is going to like it. It brings up *their* junk.

In *The Four Agreements*, Don Miguel Ruiz says when people have something to negative to say, it usually has nothing to do with you. It's about them, their perspective and their view of life. Remembering this concept will make it easier for you to keep moving forward.

Fear of Success

Fear of success? I wondered how we could be afraid of success? Isn't that what we want?

I was taken through a visualization exercise that helped me to see this. We imagined a framed picture with ourselves and the people closest to us - as we are now - at our current level of success. Try it. Got it? Then we did the exercise again. But this time we imagined the portrait, with ourselves and the people closest to us, once we had achieved our dream life. It was interesting for me to see how the picture in the frame changed. I found myself apart from everyone else because of the thoughts that came up. *Will they think I have changed? Will they not like me anymore?* These are things that I was not aware of - I was not conscious of. Could it be that I was subconsciously holding myself back to not be separated? Is this something that you've ever considered? Fear of success can also be fear of separation.

One of my favorite quotes from author and lecturer, Marianne Williamson, says **"Our deepest fear is not that we are**

inadequate. Our deepest fear is that we are powerful beyond measure." **"We ask ourselves, *who am I to be brilliant – gorgeous – talented - fabulous?* Actually, who are you *not* to be?"** **"Your playing small does not serve the world."** There is nothing enlightened about shrinking so that other people won't feel insecure around you. We are all meant to shine. As we let our own light shine, we unconsciously give those around us permission to do the same. As we are liberated from our own fear, our presence automatically liberates others.

Such a tall order, when we are stuck in our own thoughts. So how do we get out of fear and into action? One thing helps me time and time again. Curiosity.

The Cure for Fear

Consider this. When we are afraid, it's usually because we are worried about the outcome. If you approach any situation with a spirit of curiosity, it is so much easier to act in spite of and often times without fear, because you are not emotionally attached to the outcome. You just want to see what will happen.

When I try something new, I like to think of it like a science experiment. I form a hypothesis - *I think _____ is going to happen when I _____.* My goal is to be curious about what is going to happen when I test my hypotheses with action. Is this hypothesis - the statement about what I think is going to happen - true or not? If it doesn't happen, I don't get all bent out of shape and start crying. I don't think the world is coming to an end or that everybody is out to get me.   I just say, *The hypothesis was not proven* or *The hypothesis was false.*   With curiosity, I may repeat the action again adjusting some of the parameters.   Or I may formulate a different hypothesis based on the information/feedback I received from doing the experiment the first time.   I can keep doing this until I find success.

The next time you know there is something you need to do for yourself or for your business, look through the lens of a scientist. Ask yourself, *what do I think will happen?* If you're in a room of people, be curious. *I wonder who these people are around me? I wonder if they will understand if I tell them what I do? Will they ask me questions?* Using that approach turns off emotion enough for you to get into action. You're just being curious.

I wonder what would happen if...

Faith

Be clear about what you want and why you want it. The *how* will come.

It's like driving through a heavy fog. You know that you're on the road, you know what your destination is and you also know that if you just keep driving, the road will continue to reveal itself. You may not be able to see 10 feet ahead of you because of the fog but you just know that if you keep driving little by little, the road will reveal itself. That's really what faith is about, taking the next step and knowing that the road will be revealed to you as you keep moving forward.

We are constantly searching for evidence that something is true or possible, and we tend to look at our past for that evidence. We look to see if we've done it before – were we successful? But the problem is that we also see our failures as evidence. Often we make them mean, *Well, I haven't been able to do it in the past, so I can't do it now.* On the flip side, faith means, *Okay, I have these experiences in the past and I know that this doesn't work... so what am I going to do next time? What am I going to do differently?* Faith refuses to accept that a past failure means you will be unsuccessful in the future. It uses evidence as information for the next attempt. *Okay, maybe this wasn't the best way of accomplishing that goal. How else can I approach this?*

You are never given a vision to do something that you will not also be provided the means to achieve. Often, that means you will go through experiences in order to be able to relate to others. Your life lessons will teach you what to do in similar situations in the future. If you've ever been through a bad experience, you now know what to do or what not to do in that situation. But many of us take that negative experience and say, *Whoa, I shouldn't ever try that again.* We stop. And we get stuck.

The most successful people have faith that the dream and vision was given specifically to them and they will be given the tools, the people, the resources, and the experiences to successfully achieve that goal. Believing nothing is a loss and everything is a teacher, makes it easier to step out on faith and keep going. Are you willing to be courageous for your vision?

CHAPTER 7

How To Stay Motivated Through Challenges, Plateaus, And Setbacks

Everything that has happened in your life, is for a reason. It has equipped you to do exactly what you're supposed to do in this world - to share your experiences. It wasn't until a friend shared this beautiful story with me, that I fully realized why I had gone through my particular journeys.

The story is called "The Teacup."

> There was a couple who used to go to England to shop in the beautiful stores. They both liked antiques and pottery and especially teacups. This was their twenty-fifth wedding anniversary.
>
> One day in this beautiful shop they saw a beautiful teacup. They said, "May we see that? We've never seen one quite so beautiful." As the lady handed it to them, suddenly the teacup spoke.
>
> "You don't understand," it said. "I haven't always been a teacup. There was a time when I was red and I was clay." My master took me and rolled me and patted me over and over and I yelled out, "let me alone", but he only smiled, "Not yet."
>
> "Then I was placed on a spinning wheel," the teacup said, "and suddenly I was spun around and around and around. Stop it! I'm getting dizzy!" I screamed. But the

master only nodded and said, 'Not yet."

Then he put me in the oven. I never felt such heat. I wondered why he wanted to burn me, and I yelled and knocked at the door. I could see him through the opening and I could read his lips as He shook his head, "Not yet."

Finally the door opened, he put me on the shelf, and I began to cool. "There, that's better," I said. And he brushed and painted me all over. The fumes were horrible. I thought I would gag. "Stop it, stop it!" I cried. He only nodded, "Not yet."

Then suddenly he put me back into the oven, not like the first one. This was twice as hot and I knew I would suffocate. I begged. I pleaded. I screamed. I cried. All the time I could see him through the opening nodding his head saying, "Not yet."

Then I knew there wasn't any hope. I would never make it. I was ready to give up. But the door opened and he took me out and placed me on the shelf. One hour later he handed me a mirror and said, "Look at yourself." And I did. I said, "That's not me; that couldn't be me. It's beautiful. I'm beautiful."

"I want you to remember, then," he said, "I know it hurts to be rolled and patted, but if I had left you alone, you'd have dried up. I know it made you dizzy to spin around on the wheel, but if I had stopped, you would have crumbled. I knew it hurt and was hot and disagreeable in the oven, but if I hadn't put you there, you would have cracked. I know the fumes were bad when I brushed and painted you all over, but if I hadn't done that, you never would have hardened; you would not have had any color in your life. And if I hadn't put you back in that second oven, you wouldn't survive for very long because the hardness would not have held. Now you are a finished product. You are what I had in mind when I first began with you."

-Author Unknown

Challenges

Sometimes it's easy to look at life and all of its ups and downs and wonder why me? Arnold Schwarzenegger says, **"When you go through hardships and decide not to surrender, that is strength."** The challenges are necessary to build the strength you need to be ready for the end goal.

In order to build muscle, it has to be broken down first. As you lift the weight, if the resistance is greater than what the muscles are already able to tolerate, microfibers tear in the muscle. When they heal, they build up bigger and stronger than they were before. If the resistance is not greater-if the challenge is not greater than they are already capable of handling, no change in strength will occur.

This is the same process that happens in our life and in our business. If we allow ourselves to use hardships, challenges, setbacks, we can grow. Challenges in weight loss allowed me to see where I could make changes. Struggling through some aspect of business made me ready to take on bigger challenges and prepare me for success.

Plateaus

Traditionally, a plateau is thinking that whatever you were

doing has stopped working because little change can be seen. The way I see it, plateaus are the process of allowing results to catch up with new thoughts. Too many people quit just before they reach the breakthrough - the point in which conscious action becomes habit - and say they failed. Please understand that the "secret sauce" to your success is still at work in the background during those times. Beliefs and mindsets are trying to catch up, preparing for explosive growth.

I struggled to lose those first 50 pounds. It was a conscious effort - always monitoring, always watching, always checking myself. I had some flexibility, but I was rigid about watching my weight, counting points (calories) and exercising. I was working out hours a day to lose that weight. Keeping it off was also a struggle. But as I continued to read, study and learn about managing my mind and examining my thoughts and beliefs about myself, my results improved as a byproduct. Those last 30 pounds flew off so fast I couldn't stop, even I had wanted to. Even with less exercise and adding the "forbidden foods" to my pantry! The chips sat there for weeks because I had changed my mindset about them. My thoughts about food and my "self" were the issue and changing my thoughts led to different behaviors.

As you build your business, there will be a process of building momentum and learning new skills. Then you will implement those skills and receive feedback. Sometimes you will feel like, *Yes! I'm getting the hang of it.* And other times, you might feel stuck. It's normal. On the other side of that resistance is *Unstoppable Success.* Just keep going.

Steven Pressfield talks about resistance in his book, *The War of Art*. He said that resistance **"is greatest when the finish line is in sight"**. When we say the last few pounds are the hardest to lose, we are only focused on the actions that it took to work towards that goal. We don't address the thoughts and the beliefs behind the plateau.

Rest if you must, but whatever you do, don't quit. – TaVona Denise

Setbacks

We all have them. When everything seems to be going so well, then-boom! The unexpected strikes, sending us two steps backward. How do you keep moving forward when setbacks occur? Remember we were talking about thoughts, perceptions and opinions about the situation? I have learned to ask myself the question, *what's perfect about this?* This helps me shift out of blame and despair to optimism and insight. Because if you remember the concept of *pronoia,* that the universe is conspiring to support you, all of this - the good, the bad and the ugly - is just a part of the plan.

If we get caught up in thinking success is a straight line and should be easy, when challenges come our way and setbacks occur, we get stuck and quit. We blame the program, the system, the teacher. If we really understood that success is more of a crooked path, we would embrace it, knowing that it means we are on our way, that the obstacles we face as we go through change prepare us for what is ahead.

Think about the last time you drove to a friend's house. You didn't just leave your house, drive in a straight line and voilà! You're there. No. There were probably some turns, red lights and maybe even some traffic along the way. You didn't stop and turn the car around, did you? More likely, you chalked it up as a part of the journey and kept going until you reached your destination.

It happened to me during the photo shoot for this book cover. There was *a lot* of traffic, which is not unusual for Atlanta. I was going to an unfamiliar place, but I had plugged the address into the GPS. After fighting traffic, I got to a road that was clearly a part of the directions, but had been blocked off. I turned around, unsure what to do, as I was in unfamiliar territory and unsure about an alternate route. The GPS kept trying to take me down that street. I'll admit, I was a little worried, because I didn't know another way, but I was determined to get to my destination and eventually, the GPS rerouted. Life is the same way. Can we keep moving forward in spite of obstacles? Can we become *unstoppable*?

Tips for Staying Motivated

Remember to find your *why*. Keep that in front of you. Make sure your *why* evokes an emotion that keeps you pushing through. Use leverage with yourself. You know what motivates you. You know what you need to do to encourage yourself to move forward through the steps - through the fire.

Remember to honor smaller victories. Sometimes we get discouraged because we think, *Oh, no! I still haven't hit this goal.* Instead, look at how far you've come and what you've already accomplished rather than *I have so far to go* or *I'm not there yet.*

Choose the thoughts that support your success rather than sabotage it. Your perception about your circumstances and what has happened ultimately creates your results. Choosing thoughts that make you feel good is a great way to stay motivated.

Seek insight from your mentor, coach or mastermind group. Is there something that you can tweak in your strategy or process that will help to streamline things for you? This is part of the process that we go through on our way to success.

Surround yourself with people who are fired up - people who are excited about life and the direction that they're headed. Place yourself near people who want to take you with them. Drive and energy are contagious. Do you want to be touched by negative energy, or do you want to be inspired to move towards your goal?

Finally, take stock and check in with yourself. Are you still working the plan? There's no judgment and nothing to be ashamed of – just notice. From that awareness, you decide to make a change or not. Just be honest with yourself.

CONCLUSION

I'm a sprinter, so climbing hills on a bike are not my favorite. But my cycling club likes to go riding in the North Georgia mountains. Hogpen Gap, part of the Tour de Georgia, is a 7-mile climb. Lance Armstrong has even ridden up this mountain.

The first time I attempted to climb Hogpen, I was a newer cyclist. I only reached a little over halfway up the mountain. I stopped and I waited for everyone to come back down. It bothered me. I didn't make it to the top. The pain and my thoughts got the best of me. The next chance I had to go up that mountain, I was *determined* I would get to the top without stopping - and it was intense. My legs were in pain. My heart felt like it was going to explode. Though is was physically painful and my brain wanted to stop, my heart rate monitor told me I was not in serious danger.

I had a lot of time to think during that climb since it took an hour to reach the peak. This is what I learned during that climb to the top – you will need thoughts that support your goal because you will want to quit. I chose the thoughts, *I know I've gotten to this point before. I'm in much better shape than I was then. I know how to handle the bike better.*

You will need to learn how to pace yourself. I didn't want to go out there all gung-ho, burn myself out, then stop. If you are willing to do whatever it takes to be in the game for the long haul, pace yourself. And breathe. It slows down the heart rate, calms you down, and gives you something to focus on.

Anticipate the downhill. Knowing that this climb was the work that I put in, I also knew I would soon be rewarded with an exciting and fast downhill. The downhill is the freedom we're all striving for. Anticipating the downhill - the freedom - helps us to keep going day after day.

One more step.

One more step.

We become unstoppable.

The success we seek, that we are working so hard for, is on the other side of that mountain before us.

If you are still on this earth, you are meant to do something – to walk your purpose. Will you step into your greatness or just let the time pass? Yes, there may be a lot of steps on the journey to success and it may not always be pleasant. Some will make it, others won't. But those with a burning desire for to do something great in their life and achieve Unstoppable Success, will find ways to stay motivated.

Throughout the journey, the greatest lesson I have learned is that success is 80% mental and 20% skill. Whether it was losing a significant amount of weight and keeping it off or building a business that fit the lifestyle I dreamed of for myself, the hardest part was getting my mind right. The principles are the same. You get to decide what success looks like and can put specific things in place to help you get there.

We know that we should eat when we're hungry, stop when we're full and move more. We know that we should network and make sales calls. But when we're not doing the things that we know will directly contribute to ourselves, to our success, it's time to look inward.

Your *mind* above anything else is the most powerful tool you have in creating success during this journey. Learn how to manage it and nothing and no one in the world can stop you from getting what you want. It may take a while longer and the path may look a little different than you anticipated, but keep the faith because the truth of the matter is, if you don't quit, you *will* win.

INVITATION

I would love to hear from you. Please email me at Unstoppable@TaVonaDenise.com with your thoughts, questions about coaching or anything I discussed here. To stay connected and be the first to know when new workshops, books or programs are available, hop over to www.TaVonaDenise.com and sign up for the mailing list. I am there weekly providing insight and information to help you reach your goals. You can also connect with me on social media.

To your *Unstoppable Success!* – **TaVona Denise**

THANKS

When you edify others, they will stand up and support your dreams.

I have been so amazed and thankful throughout this process. People I have known forever, and others for only a short while have stepped up, given of their time, energy, and expertise, to make my dream a reality.

I know I don't know it all, and am grateful to each of you who have shared stories, resources and information. To those who have given talent - and to those who have given advice - helping me complete this project, you know who you are. I am forever grateful.

ABOUT THE AUTHOR

Atlanta-based business accelerator, life coach, and avid cyclist, TaVona Denise lives by the motto, "Success is 80% mental, and 20% skill." With certifications in life, weight, and wellness coaching, her specialty is helping new entrepreneurs move past fear and overwhelm to start their own thriving business.

It wasn't until TaVona found the world of coaching and mentoring that she was able to successfully lose 80 pounds and maintain that loss, become an award-winning athlete, and build the business that would eventually provide the lifestyle she wanted.

TaVona teaches entrepreneurs the steps she used to create lasting success as a lifestyle, in weight loss and business. She believes there would be less addiction in the world if people were courageous enough to walk in their purpose. She is on a mission to help clients find their zone of genius, shut out the voices of fear and critics, and create income by making a difference.

MOTIVATIONAL QUOTES

If you couldn't tell, I love motivational and inspirational quotes and since I couldn't put them all in the book, I thought I would share some more of them with you here. Enjoy!

When you need a boost or a kick in the rear, read these. If you have a favorite motivational quote, drop me a line at Unstoppable@TaVonaDenise.com I'd love to hear them.

The greatest good you can do for another is not just to share your riches, but reveal to him his own. -Benjamin Disraeli

When I dare to be powerful, to use my strength in the service of my vision, it becomes less and less important whether I am afraid. -Audre Lorde

Failure is a part of the process. It's how we find out who we really are. -Stephen Cope

The only place success comes before work is in the dictionary. -Unknown

The pathway to your greatest potential is straight through your greatest fear. -Greg Groschel

Life doesn't always let you see the path, but it doesn't mean you shouldn't keep walking -Unknown

It is not the information you get, but the information you use that makes a difference. -TaVona Denise

If it doesn't challenge you, it won't change you. -Fred Devito

Just because something fails, doesn't mean you are a failure. - TaVona Denise

The temptation to quit will be the greatest just before you're about to succeed. -Chinese Proverb

In order to fly, you must First Love Yourself -Michael Maher

Failure is a bruise, not a tattoo. -Jon Sinclair

Rule your mind, or it will rule you. -Buddah

Failure isn't falling down. Failure is staying down. -Debbie Storey

There are 7 days in a week and someday isn't one of them. - Unknown

A girl knows her limits, but a wise girl knows she has none. - Marilyn Monroe

Don't let someone dim your light, simply because it's shining in their eyes. -Unknown

SPONSORS:

Vanetta Aunray
Aunray Designs
www.AunrayDesigns.com

Veronica Boggs
Gracie's Place Assisted Living
graciesplaceassistedliving.com

Adrienne R Cash
The Story is Enough
thestoryisenough.blogspot.com

Nicole Flores
Nicky Pink & Co.
https://nickypinkandco.com

Molly Freestone
Molly Freestone, Personal Life Coach
www.mollyfreestone.com

Sharon Martin
Damsel In Defense IDP
www.mydamselpro.net/SharonM

Diana Murphy
Diana Murphy Coaching
www.dianamurphycoaching.com

Trina Newby
Women About Biz
http://www.womenaboutbiz.com

Chinenye & Kia-Marie Oparah
Raise the Bar Learning, LLC
www.raisethebarlearning.com

Tracey Russell
Filthy Clean Janitorial Services Inc.
www.filthycleanjanitorial.com

Tirah Harold Thompson
Mary Kay Cosmetics Top Achievers
www.marykay.com/tirah

Rhonda Townsend
People. Process. Profits.
www.peopleprocessprofits.com

Skye Tyler
Skye Tyler LLC
www.skyetyler.com

Sunshine Weaver
Sunshine Dezigns
www.MaryKay.com/SunshyneDezigns

Willayna Roberts Banner
R&B Global Investments Inc.

Karen M Grant
www.NursesFirst.org

Sandy Stewart
coachsandy.net

Kathy Thacker
Be Fit Now

Sundiata Alaye

Sandra O. Anderson

Jacqueline Echols

Kay Norward-Gilmore

Janice M. Neal

Elise Nichols

Lucy Roberts

Stacy Saraydar

Shekiah Flowers Stinson

Roland White

Ebonee' R. Williams

Connect with TaVona Denise on Social Media

www.Facebook.com/TaVonaDenise

www.Instagram.com/TaVonaDenise

www.Periscope.tv/TaVonaDenise

www.Twitter.com/TaVonaDenise

www.Pinterest.com/TaVonaDenise

www.YouTube.com/TaVonaDenise

www.ingramcontent.com/pod-product-compliance
Lightning Source LLC
Chambersburg PA
CBHW072204090426
42740CB00012B/2380